1·2·3 Draw

Knights, Castles, and Dragons

A step
by step
guide

by
Freddie
Levin

PEEL PRODUCTIONS, INC.

Before you begin...

You will need:

- a pencil
- an eraser
- a pencil sharpener
- a ruler for drawing straight edges
- lots of paper (recycle and re-use)
- colored pencils for finished drawings
- a folder for saving work
- a comfortable place to draw
- good light

Now let's begin...!

Published by Peel Productions, Inc.
Printed in China

Library of Congress Cataloging-in-Publication Data

Levin, Freddie.

1-2-3 draw knights, castles, and dragons: a step by step guide / by Freddie Levin. p. cm.
Includes index.
Summary: Simple instructions for drawing dragons, knights and their weapons, and castles and the people who lived in them.
ISBN 0-939217-43-0
1. Knights and knighthood in art--Juvenile literature. 2. Dragons in art--Juvenile literature. 3. Castles in art--Juvenile literature. 4. Drawing--Technique--Juvenile literature. [1. Knights and knighthood in art. 2. Dragons in art. 3. Castles in art. 4. Drawing--Technique.] I. Title: Knights, castles, and dragons. II. Title: One-two-three draw knights, castles, and dragons. III. Title.

NC825.K54 L49 2001
743'.8--dc21   2001036642Ò

Distributed to the trade and art markets in North America by

NORTH LIGHT BOOKS,
an imprint of F&W Publications, Inc.
4700 East Galbraith Road
Cincinnati, OH 45236

(800) 289-0963

Contents

Important Drawing Tips:

1 Draw lightly (SKETCH!) at first, so you can erase extra lines.

2 Practice, practice, practice.

3 Have fun drawing knights, castles

and dragons!

Basic Shapes

The drawings in this book start with three basic shapes. Learn these shapes and practice drawing them.

 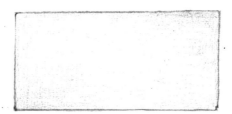

A **square** has four equal sides.

A **rectangle** has four sides; two sides are longer.

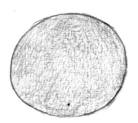  

A **circle** is perfectly round.

An **oval** is a squashed circle.

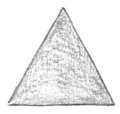 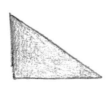 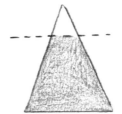 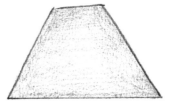

A **triangle** has three points and three sides.   A **trapezoid** is a triangle with one point cut off.

The more you practice drawing these shapes, the easier it will be.
Remember: Draw lightly!

Note to parents and teachers:
I have found it helpful in working with very young children with poorly developed motor control to have them begin their drawings by tracing a small cardboard cutout of an oval or circle.

Basic Person, Front View

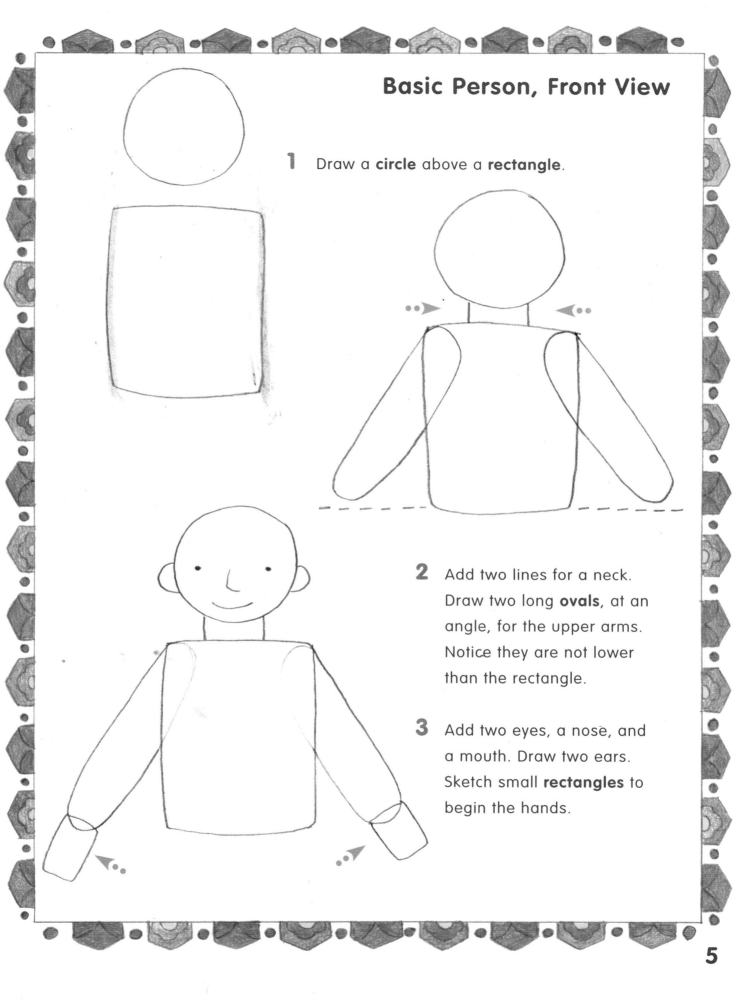

1 Draw a **circle** above a **rectangle**.

2 Add two lines for a neck. Draw two long **ovals**, at an angle, for the upper arms. Notice they are not lower than the rectangle.

3 Add two eyes, a nose, and a mouth. Draw two ears. Sketch small **rectangles** to begin the hands.

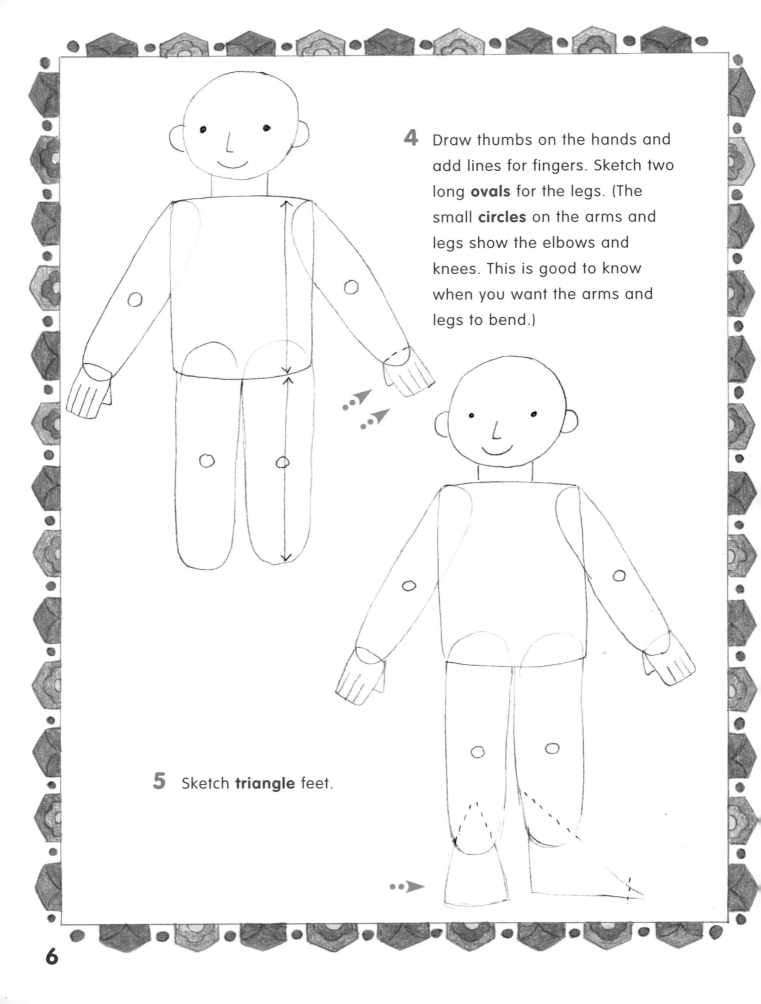

4 Draw thumbs on the hands and add lines for fingers. Sketch two long **ovals** for the legs. (The small **circles** on the arms and legs show the elbows and knees. This is good to know when you want the arms and legs to bend.)

5 Sketch **triangle** feet.

6 To finish your person, erase extra lines. The next few pages will show you how to turn the basic person into different people.

Facial Expressions:
LOOK at these different expressions! Practice drawing them.

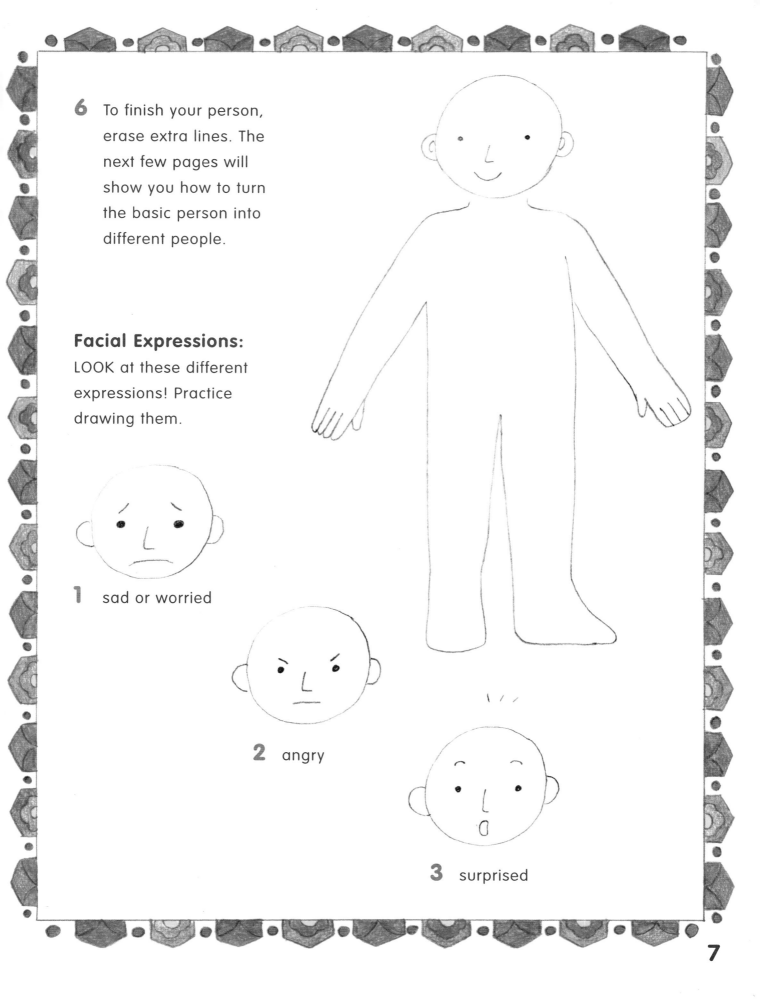

1 sad or worried

2 angry

3 surprised

The King

1 Start with your **basic person, front view** (see pages 5-7). Draw one hand in a holding position (see page 20).

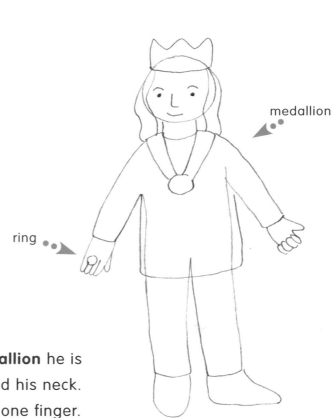

see page 20

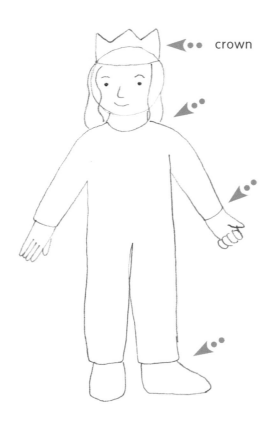

crown

2 Draw a **crown**. Add long hair. Draw clothing lines at the neck, feet and hands.

medallion

ring

3 Draw the **medallion** he is wearing around his neck. Add a **ring** on one finger.

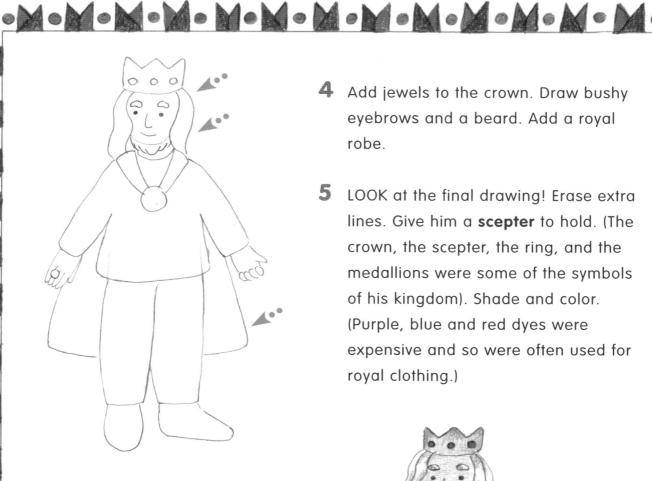

4 Add jewels to the crown. Draw bushy eyebrows and a beard. Add a royal robe.

5 LOOK at the final drawing! Erase extra lines. Give him a **scepter** to hold. (The crown, the scepter, the ring, and the medallions were some of the symbols of his kingdom). Shade and color. (Purple, blue and red dyes were expensive and so were often used for royal clothing.)

scepter

During the Middle Ages (500 A.D to 1500 A.D.), Europe was divided into many small nations constantly at war. A king owned all the land in his kingdom. He gave some of his land to barons who then swore loyalty to the king. The barons helped the king fight the kings of other nations. Sometimes the king had to keep his own barons from fighting with each other. It was not easy to be a king during the Middle Ages.

Basic Person, Side View

1 Draw a **circle** above a **rectangle**.

2 Add two lines for the neck. Draw two long, thin **ovals** for the arms. Notice the angle.

3 Draw a **triangle** for the nose. Add an eye, a mouth, and an ear. Draw two **rectangles** to begin the hands.

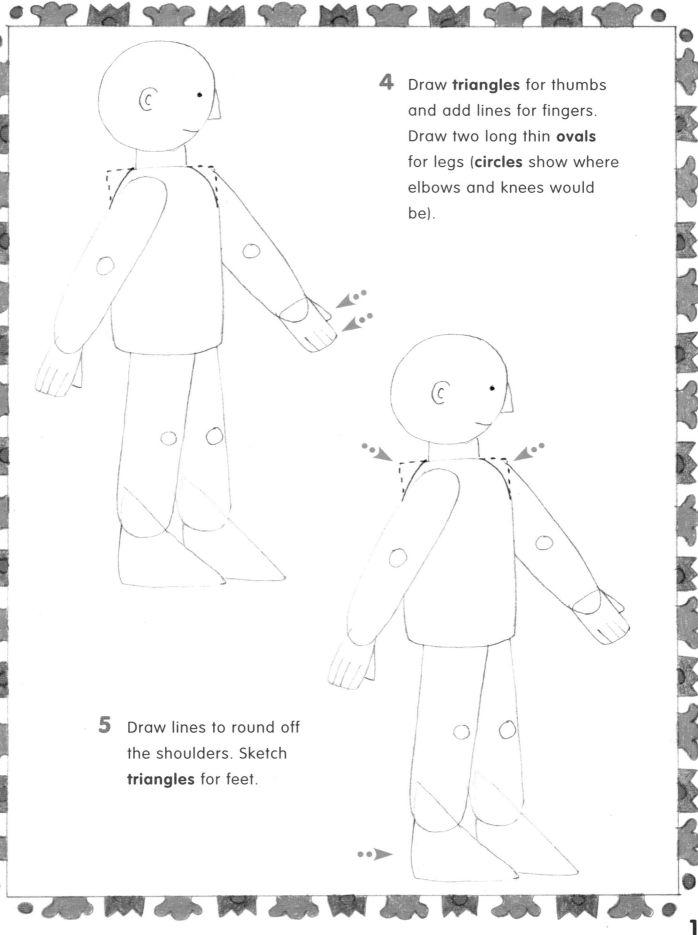

4 Draw **triangles** for thumbs and add lines for fingers. Draw two long thin **ovals** for legs (**circles** show where elbows and knees would be).

5 Draw lines to round off the shoulders. Sketch **triangles** for feet.

6 LOOK at the final drawing! Erase extra lines. You are now ready to turn the basic person into different people.

Facial Expressions: LOOK at these different expressions! Practice drawing them.

1 angry

2 sad

3 surprised

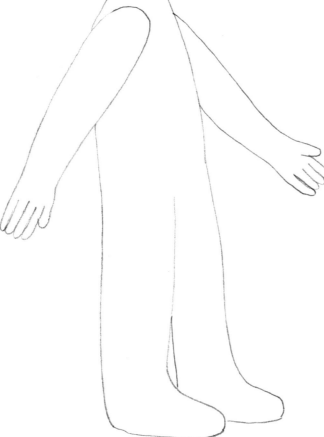

A Princess

A princess is the daughter of a king and queen. During the Middle Ages, she was expected to learn how to manage a large household, use herbs for medicines, embroider, dance and play a musical instrument. She had to be a gracious hostess as well.

hennin

kirtle

1 Start with your **basic person, side view** (see pages 10-12).

2 Draw a **triangular** hat called a **hennin** (HEN in). Add clothing lines at the neck and wrists. Draw a long, flowing dress called a **kirtle** (KIR till).

3 Draw a flowing scarf from the tip of the hat. Draw long wavy hair. Give the princess a bead necklace.

4 LOOK at the final drawing! Erase extra lines. Shade and color. (Royalty often wore richly decorated clothing. This princess has a kirtle of embroidered stars and satin slippers.)

Basic Person, Running

1 Draw a **circle** for the head and a tilted **rectangle** for the upper body. Add neck lines. Draw the face, ear, and **triangle** nose. Add lines to round the shoulders.

2 Draw **ovals** for the upper and lower arms, bent at the elbow. Add **rectangles** for hands. Draw lines for fingers. Add a **triangle** thumb.

3 Draw upper legs and **ovals** for lower legs, bent at the knees. Add **triangle** feet.

4 LOOK at the final drawing!
Erase extra lines.

Pointing Hand:

1 Sketch a **rectangle**.

2 Add a **rectangle** finger.

3 Draw three more **rectangle**
fingers and a thumb.

4 Erase extra lines.

A Prince

A prince is the son of a king and queen. The oldest son of a king would inherit his father's land. He had to learn many skills that would help him to be a good leader when he grew up. He learned to hunt and ride and fight. Some princes also learned to read and recite long stories called ballads.

1 Draw a **basic person, running** (see pages 15-16).

2 Draw hair. Add clothing lines at neck and hands. Draw lines for the bottom of the prince's **tunic**.

tunic

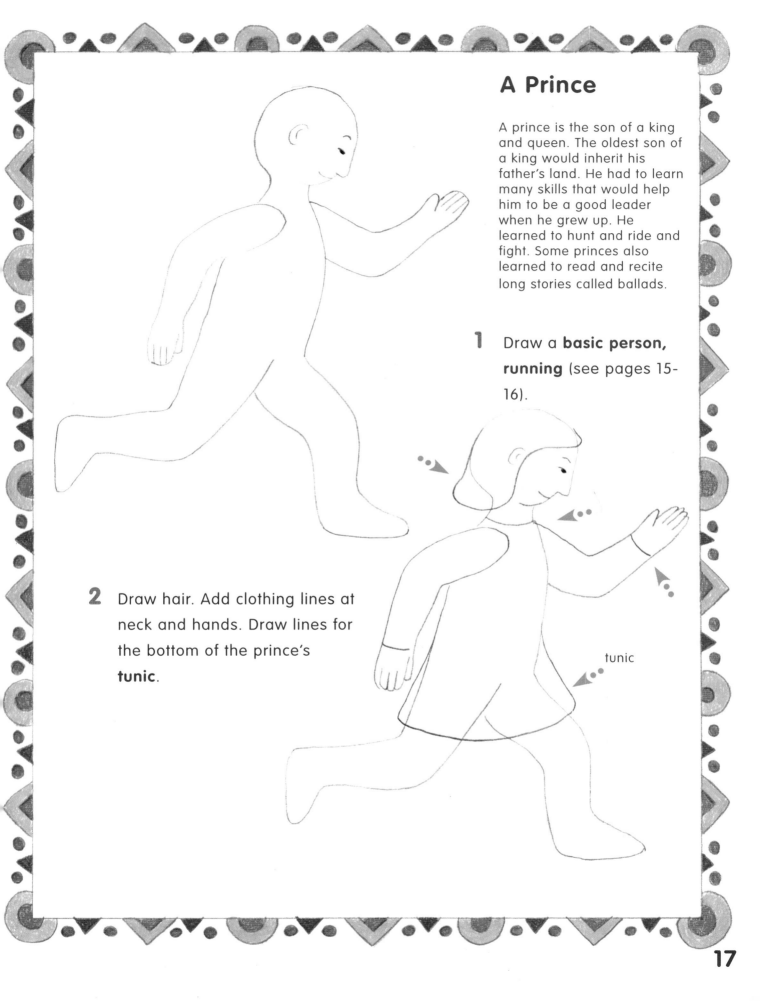

crown

belt

3 Draw a **crown** for the prince. Add a **belt** to the tunic. Draw a clothing line near the feet.

4 LOOK at the final drawing. Erase extra lines. Add some jewels to his crown. Draw the details you see. Shade and color.

Perfect prince!

Basic Person, Sitting

1 Draw a **circle** for the head and a **rectangle** for the upper body. Add a **triangle** nose. Draw the eye, ear, and mouth. Add two lines for the neck.

2 Draw long thin **ovals** for the upper and lower arms, bending at the elbow. Add a **rectangle** for the hand. Draw a thumb and lines for fingers.

3 Draw lines to round the shoulders. Draw **ovals** for the upper and lower leg, bent at the knee. Add a **triangle** for a foot.

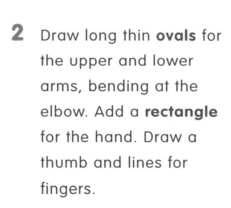

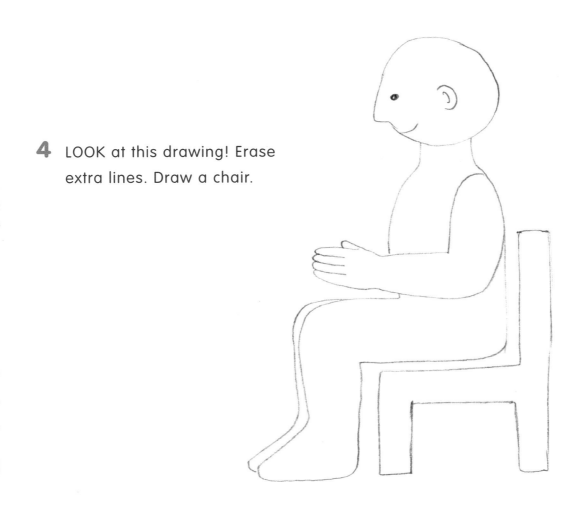

4 LOOK at this drawing! Erase extra lines. Draw a chair.

Hand Holding Something:

1 Start with a **rectangle**.

2 Add four small **ovals** for fingers.

3 Draw a thumb.

4 Erase extra lines. Draw a handle for the hand to hold.

The Queen

1 Start with a **basic person, sitting** (see pages 19-20).

2 Draw a crown. Add clothing lines at the neck and hand. Draw a long flowing skirt.

The queen was the wife of the king and the lady of the castle. She wore richly embroidered clothes and jewels to show the wealth of the kingdom. She was accomplished at sewing, music, and dancing. Her jobs included housekeeping and healing. She also helped teach her children so that they could become good kings and queens when they grew up. If the king was away on hunting trips or fighting battles, the queen was in charge of the kingdom.

3 Draw her curly hair. Add a ring. Add lines to change the chair into a throne by making the back taller and the feet bigger.

4 LOOK at the final drawing! Erase extra lines. Add jewels to her crown. Give her a necklace. Decorate the throne with jewels. Shade and color.

Castle One

Stone castles in Europe date from the 11th century. The name castle comes from the Latin word for fort or stronghold. Some were luxurious and fancy to show off the wealth of the king, but some were as bare and cold as a cave.

1 Draw two connecting **rectangles**. You may want to use a ruler to keep your lines straight.

2 Add two connecting **rectangles** on the left side. Notice, the lower **rectangle** is slightly wider.

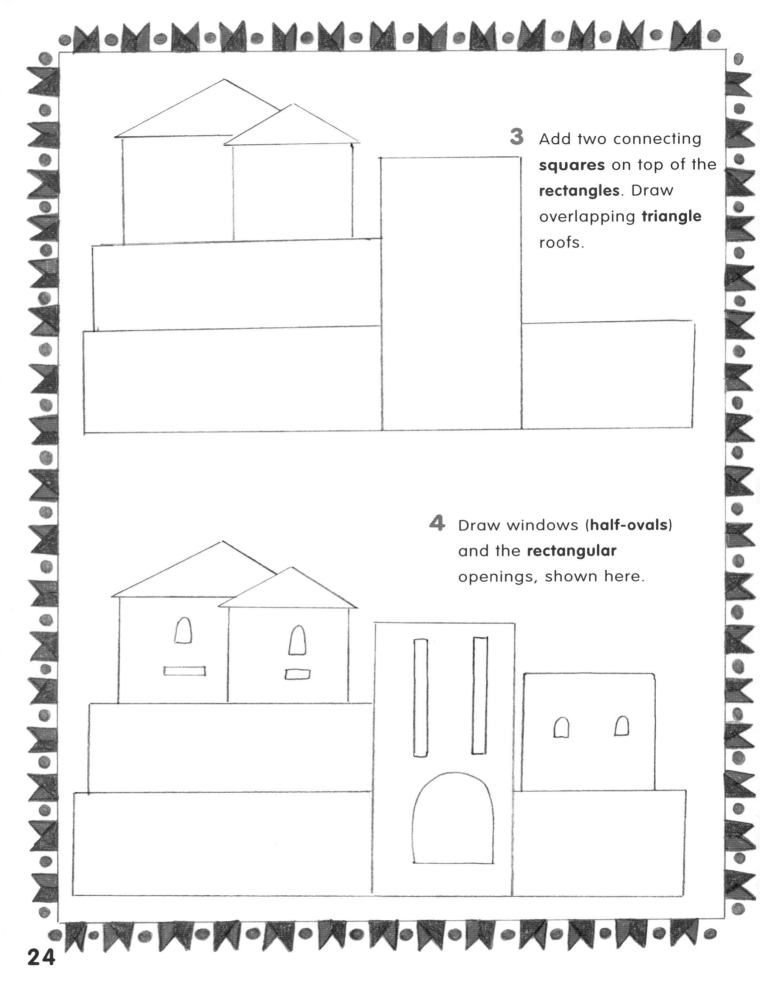

3 Add two connecting **squares** on top of the **rectangles**. Draw overlapping **triangle** roofs.

4 Draw windows (**half-ovals**) and the **rectangular** openings, shown here.

24

5 Add three more **rectangular** shapes. Draw more windows. Add iron bars (**portcullis**) to the main gate. The portcullis covers the main entrance to the castle and prevents the entrance of an enemy.

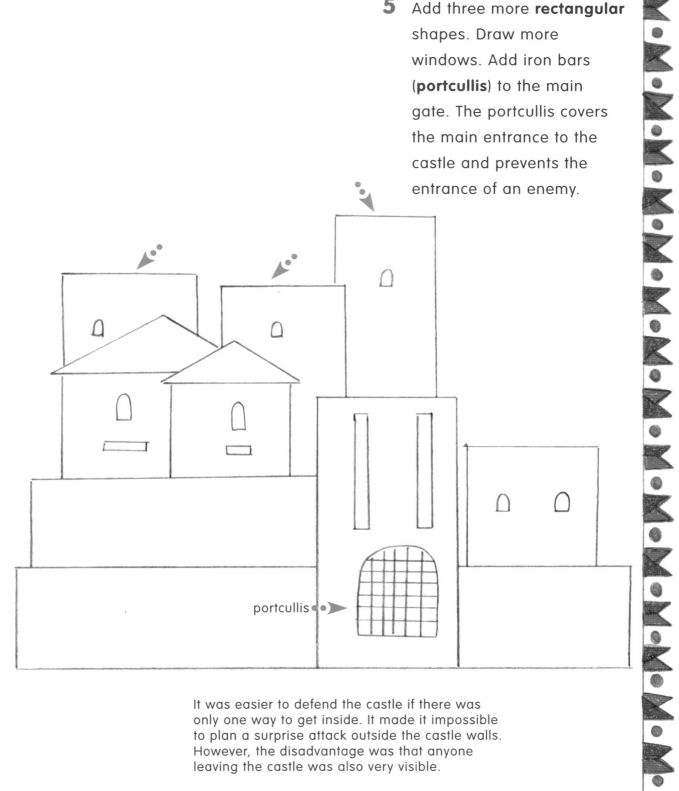

portcullis

It was easier to defend the castle if there was only one way to get inside. It made it impossible to plan a surprise attack outside the castle walls. However, the disadvantage was that anyone leaving the castle was also very visible.

6 Draw **crenelations** and **machicolations** on the castle towers. Add a road coming out of the main gate. Leave a space for the **moat**.

The forms on top of a castle tower are called **crenelations** (kren a LAY shuns). They allowed soldiers to aim down at the enemy and still have the protection of the stone walls. The overhanging openings underneath the crenelation are called **machicolations** (ma CHIK a LAY shuns) and they served the same purpose.

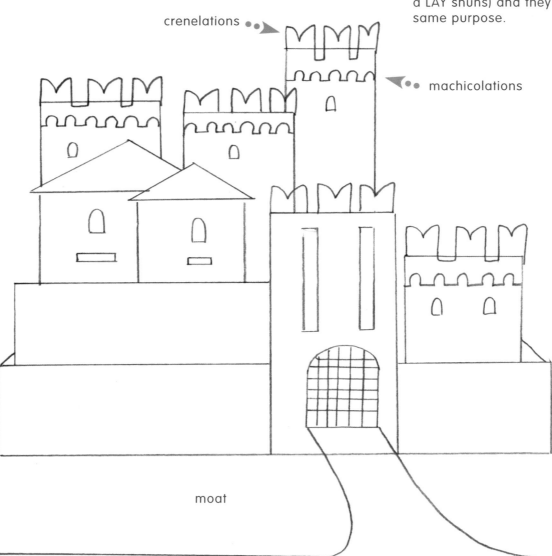

crenelations

machicolations

moat

A moat was a ditch that was dug around the castle and filled with water. The only way to get to the main gate was over a bridge. The moat kept soldiers from getting close to the castle walls.

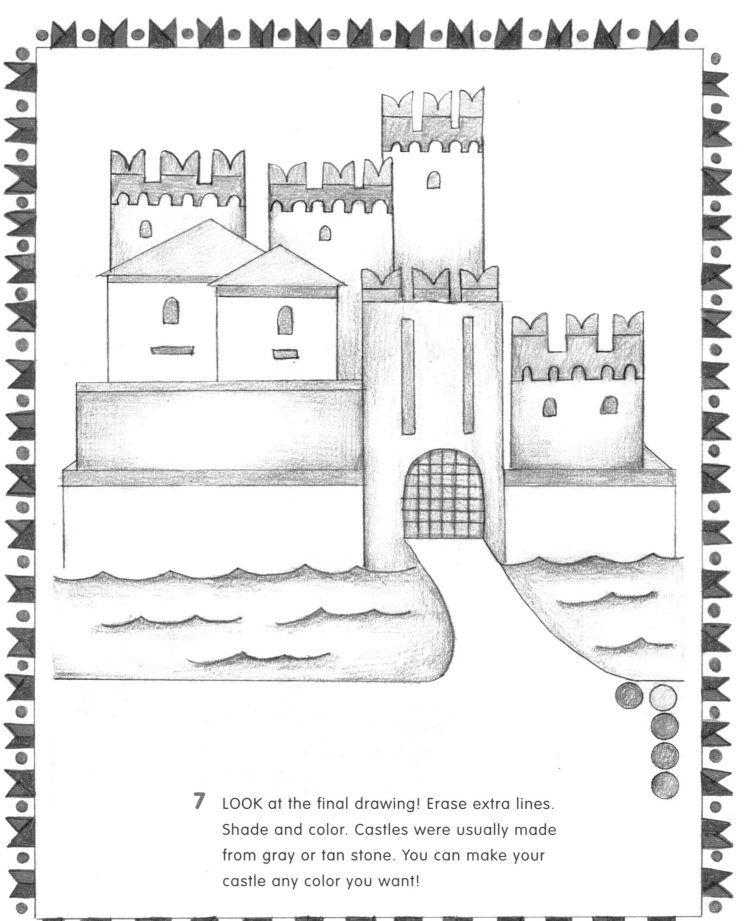

7 LOOK at the final drawing! Erase extra lines. Shade and color. Castles were usually made from gray or tan stone. You can make your castle any color you want!

Castle Two

Castles were built on foundations of natural rock. When a ditch or moat was dug, the rock was used to build the castle walls which were often eight feet thick or more. The roofs of the towers were made of sheets of lead because it was fireproof. Sometimes as many as 3,000 workers were employed to build the castle.

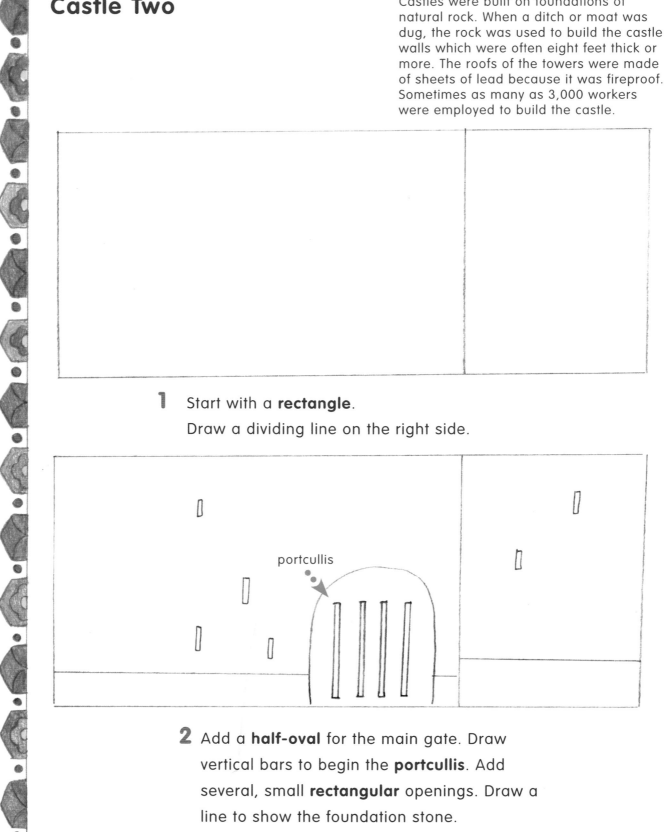

portcullis

1 Start with a **rectangle**.
Draw a dividing line on the right side.

2 Add a **half-oval** for the main gate. Draw vertical bars to begin the **portcullis**. Add several, small **rectangular** openings. Draw a line to show the foundation stone.

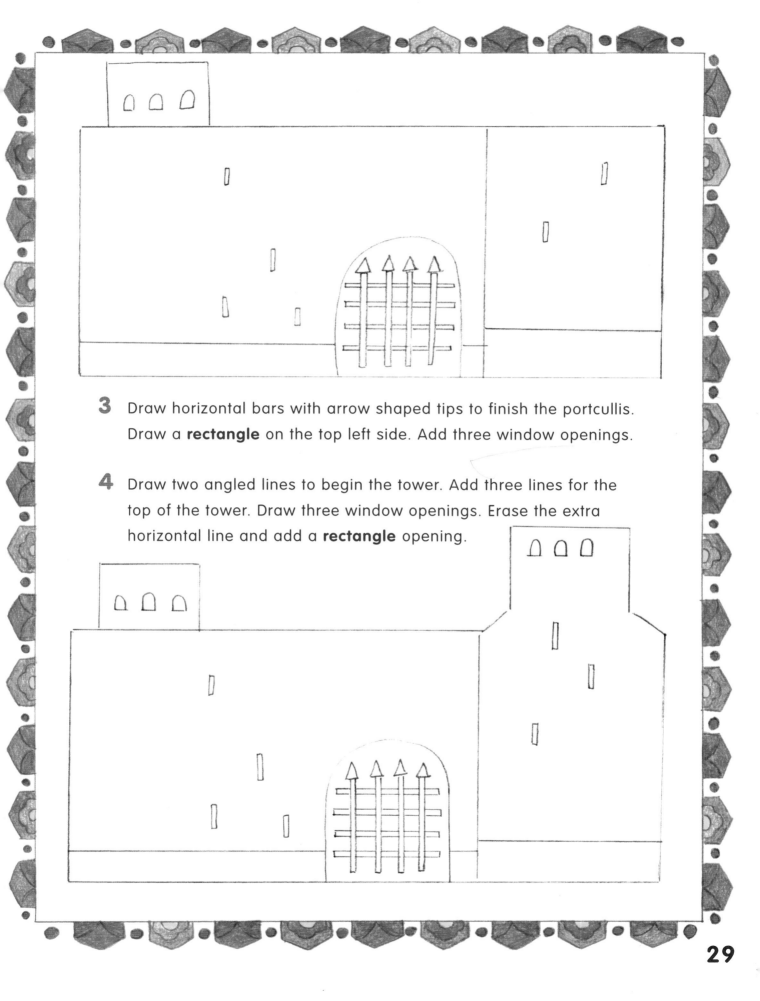

3 Draw horizontal bars with arrow shaped tips to finish the portcullis. Draw a **rectangle** on the top left side. Add three window openings.

4 Draw two angled lines to begin the tower. Add three lines for the top of the tower. Draw three window openings. Erase the extra horizontal line and add a **rectangle** opening.

5 Draw three tall **rectangles** starting on the left. Add a **triangle** roof to the one above the gate. Draw a **square** on top of the tower.

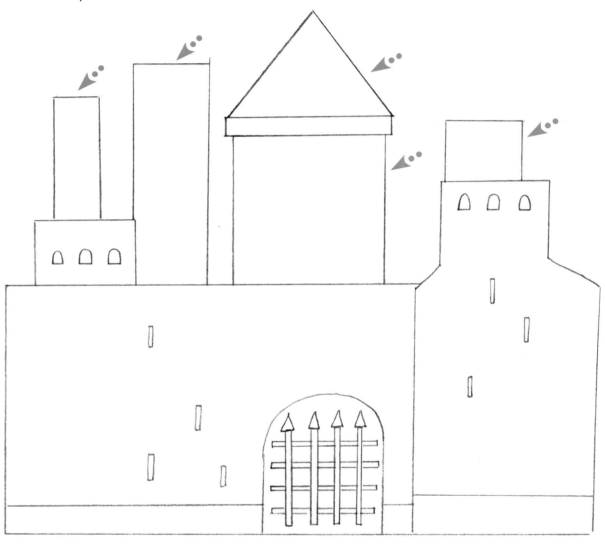

The place in the middle of the castle, where people lived, was called the "keep." It was higher than the surrounding walls. Inside, it was often decorated with richly colored weavings called 'tapestries' and beautifully carved stone.

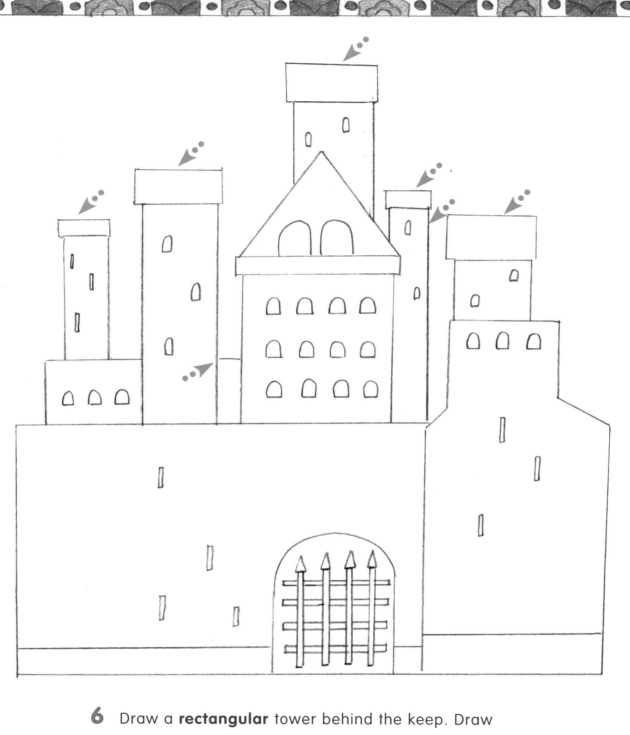

6 Draw a **rectangular** tower behind the keep. Draw another **rectangular** tower to the right of the keep. On top of each tower, draw a **rectangle**. Add a line between the second tower and the keep. Draw all the windows and openings you see.

7 Add **triangle** roofs to the tops of all the towers. Draw crenelations (see page 26) just beneath the **triangle** roofs. Add stone carving to the **triangle** roof of the middle tower—the keep.

8 LOOK at the final drawing! Erase extra lines. Shade and color. Remember that even though most real castles were made of gray or tan stone, you can make your castle any color you want.

Cool castle!

Swan

Make a swan to swim in your castle moat!

1 Sketch a **circle** for the head and an **oval** for the body.

2 Connect the **circle** and the **oval** with curving neck lines. Add tail feathers.

3 Draw an eye and a beak. Add a wing line.

4 Erase extra lines. Shade and color your swan.

Heraldry

During the Middle Ages, most people could not read. A man in a full suit of armor was not easy to identify. So each family designed a unique shield or crest. A man would wear it on the coat that covered his armor and this became his **coat of arms**. Heraldry is the study of coats of arms and family histories. These are some of the designs that were used in heraldry. Can you design one for yourself or your family?

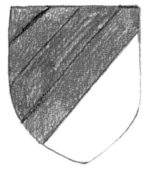

Diagonal Stripes

Chevron Stripe

Checks

Flowers and Dots *(rondels)*

Chevron and Leaf

Wavy Llines

Diagonal Stripe and Crowns

Dragon

A Knight

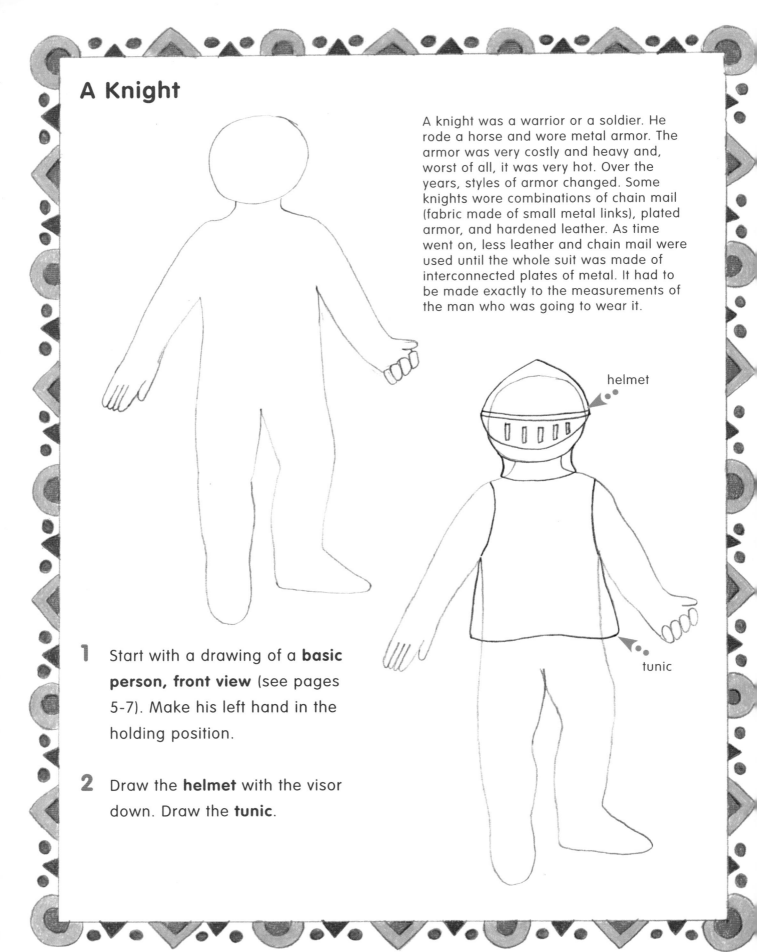

A knight was a warrior or a soldier. He rode a horse and wore metal armor. The armor was very costly and heavy and, worst of all, it was very hot. Over the years, styles of armor changed. Some knights wore combinations of chain mail (fabric made of small metal links), plated armor, and hardened leather. As time went on, less leather and chain mail were used until the whole suit was made of interconnected plates of metal. It had to be made exactly to the measurements of the man who was going to wear it.

helmet

tunic

1 Start with a drawing of a **basic person, front view** (see pages 5-7). Make his left hand in the holding position.

2 Draw the **helmet** with the visor down. Draw the **tunic**.

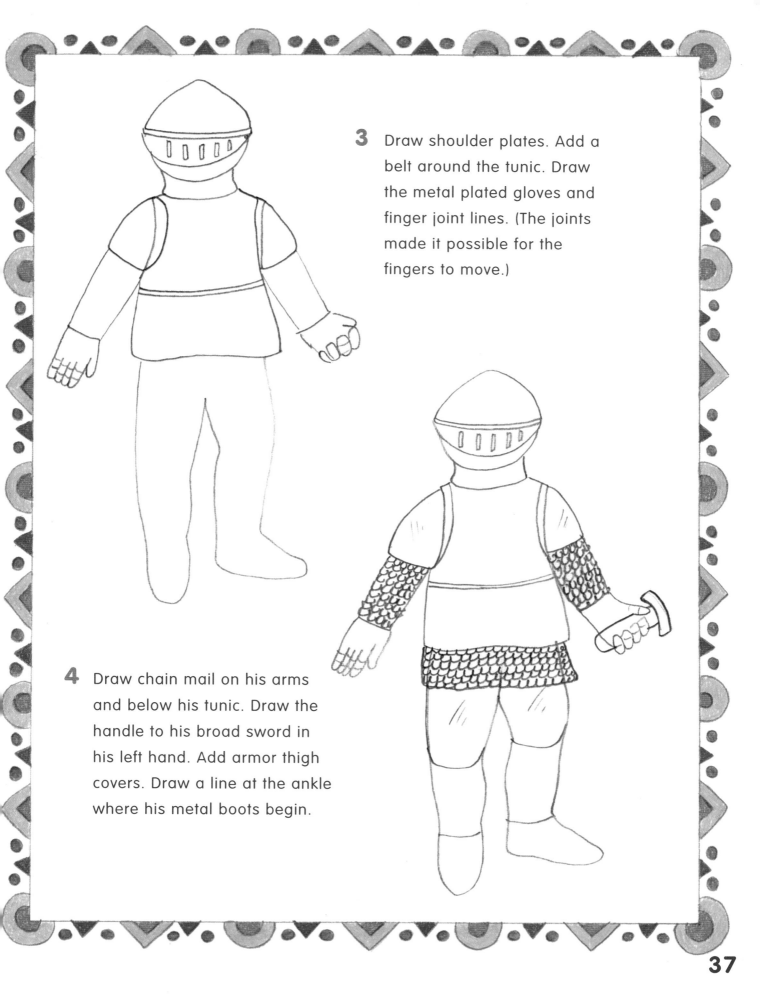

3 Draw shoulder plates. Add a belt around the tunic. Draw the metal plated gloves and finger joint lines. (The joints made it possible for the fingers to move.)

4 Draw chain mail on his arms and below his tunic. Draw the handle to his broad sword in his left hand. Add armor thigh covers. Draw a line at the ankle where his metal boots begin.

5 LOOK at the final drawing! Erase extra lines. Draw the coat of arms on his tunic. Add other details you see. Don't forget his broad sword and his boot plates—they made it possible for him to move his feet.

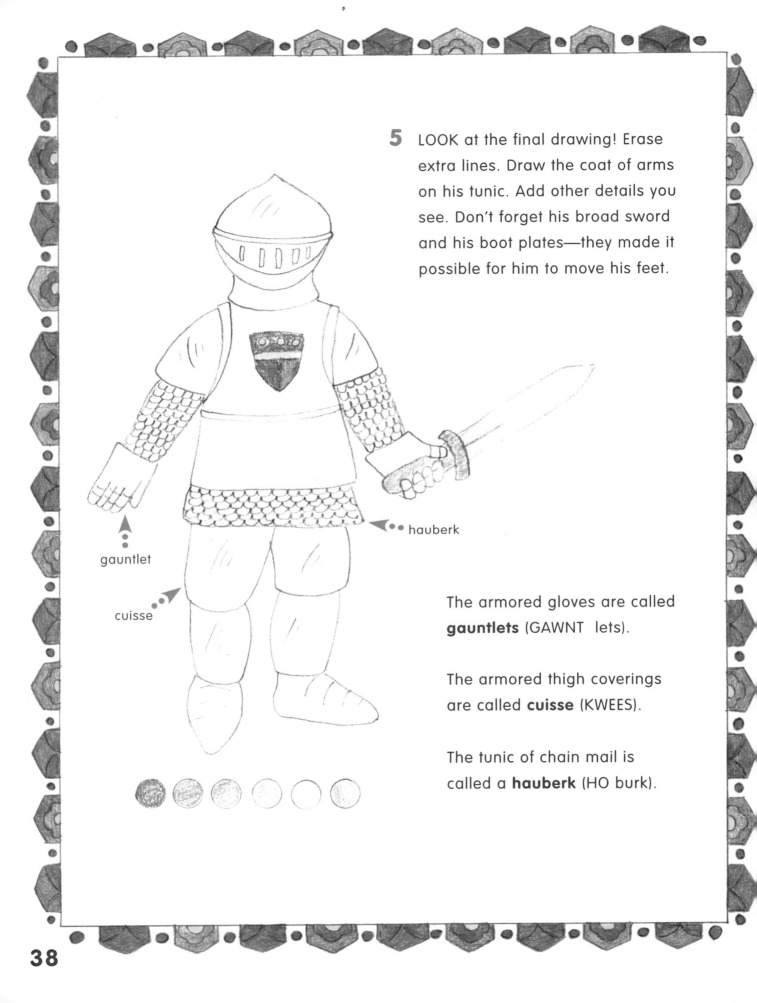

gauntlet

cuisse

hauberk

The armored gloves are called **gauntlets** (GAWNT lets).

The armored thigh coverings are called **cuisse** (KWEES).

The tunic of chain mail is called a **hauberk** (HO burk).

Horse

A knight's horse had to be big and sturdy to carry a man and all his armor into battle. Sometimes the horse also wore coat of arms and specially made armor. A well trained, valiant horse was an asset to a knight and highly valued.

1 Sketch a small **circle** for the horse's head. Sketch a big **oval** for the body.

2 Draw curved lines for the neck. Add the nose and mouth.

3 Draw two ears, an eye, and a nostril. Draw the flowing tail.

4 Draw a front and a back leg.

5 Add another front leg and
another back leg. Draw a line
for the hooves.

bridle

reins

6 Draw the **reins** and **bridle**.

7 Add a **saddle**. Erase extra lines.

saddle

You can shade and color your horse, or wait and add a rider. (Pages 42 through 44 show you how to draw a knight riding your horse.)

Knight on Horseback

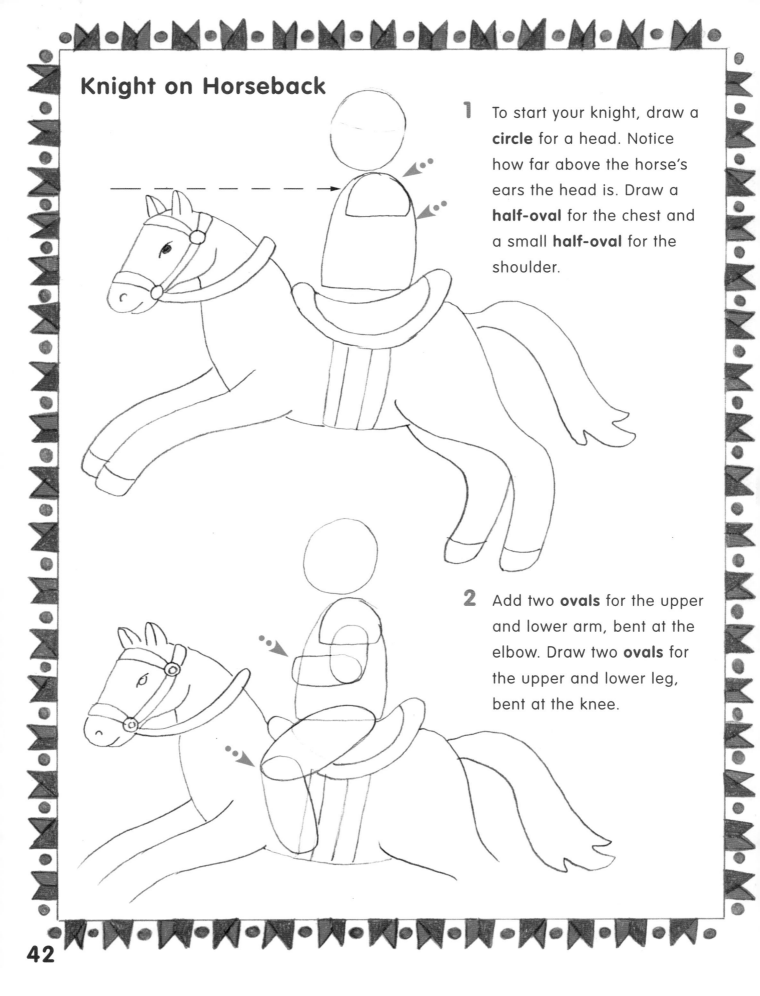

1 To start your knight, draw a **circle** for a head. Notice how far above the horse's ears the head is. Draw a **half-oval** for the chest and a small **half-oval** for the shoulder.

2 Add two **ovals** for the upper and lower arm, bent at the elbow. Draw two **ovals** for the upper and lower leg, bent at the knee.

helmet

3 Draw a **helmet** on the knight's head.
Draw a hand holding the reins. Draw feet.

43

4 LOOK at the final drawing! Erase extra lines. Draw a scene. (The castle in the background is on pages 28-33.) Shade and color.

Standing Dragon

1 Sketch a small **circle** for the dragon's head. Sketch a large **oval** for its body.

2 Add curving neck lines. Draw a nose and mouth.

3 Draw spiky scales down his neck. Draw a diamond shaped eye. Add a nostril.

The people of the Middle Ages believed many things that we do not. They believed that the Earth was flat and that the sun revolved around the Earth. They believed in the existence of the huge, fire-breathing reptiles called dragons. Many stories were told of brave knights who battled dragons to save villages, castles, or princesses.

4 Draw a front leg. Draw a back leg. Add a curving tail.

5 Draw a front foot. Draw a back foot. Add spiky scales to the long tail.

6 Draw a wing. Draw another front foot. Draw another back leg and foot.

7 Draw another wing. Add lines to the first wing. Draw claws on all four feet.

8 Draw fire coming out of his mouth. Add lines on his neck, belly and tail. Draw lots of scales on your dragon.

9 LOOK at the final drawing! Erase extra lines. Shade and color your dragon.

Dragons are imaginary and can be any color you want them to be!

Dynamite dragon!

Flying Dragon

1 Sketch a small **circle** for the head, and a big **oval** for the body. Notice the positions of the oval and the circle.

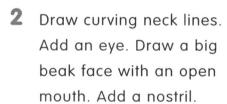

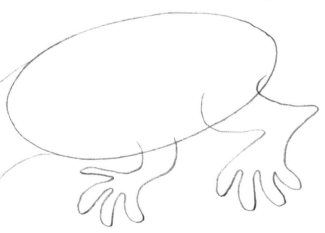

2 Draw curving neck lines. Add an eye. Draw a big beak face with an open mouth. Add a nostril.

3 Draw two front legs and feet. Draw a back leg and foot.

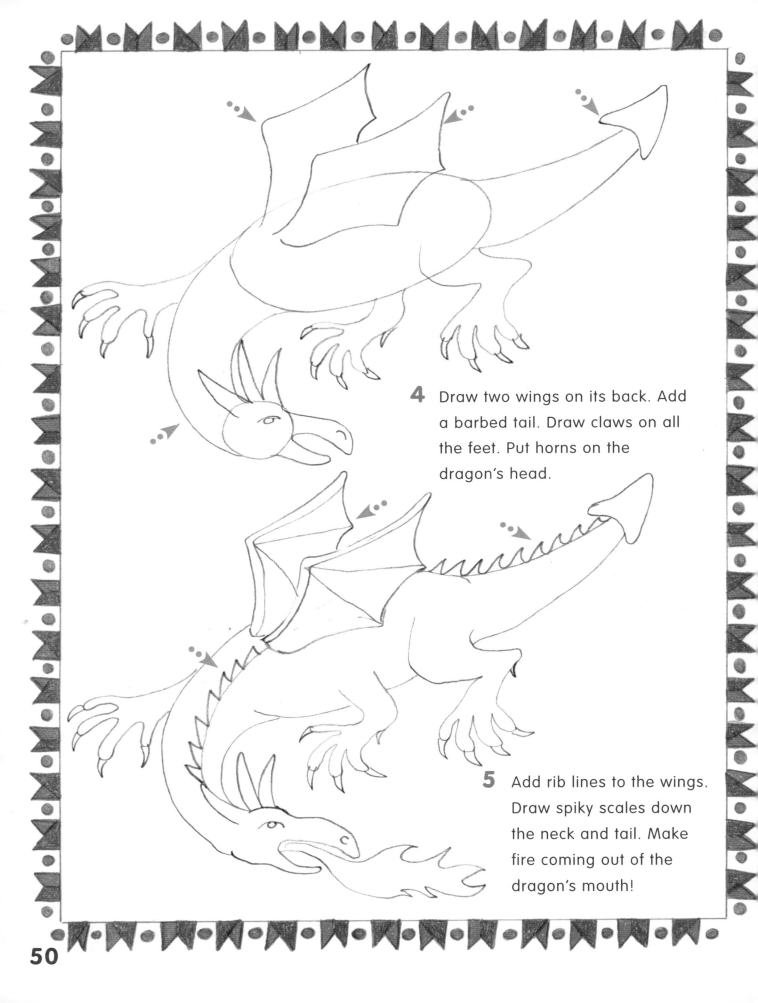

4 Draw two wings on its back. Add a barbed tail. Draw claws on all the feet. Put horns on the dragon's head.

5 Add rib lines to the wings. Draw spiky scales down the neck and tail. Make fire coming out of the dragon's mouth!

50

6 LOOK at the final drawing! Erase extra lines. Add details. Shade and color your dragon. Make a background scene with a knight battling the dragon!

51

Weapons

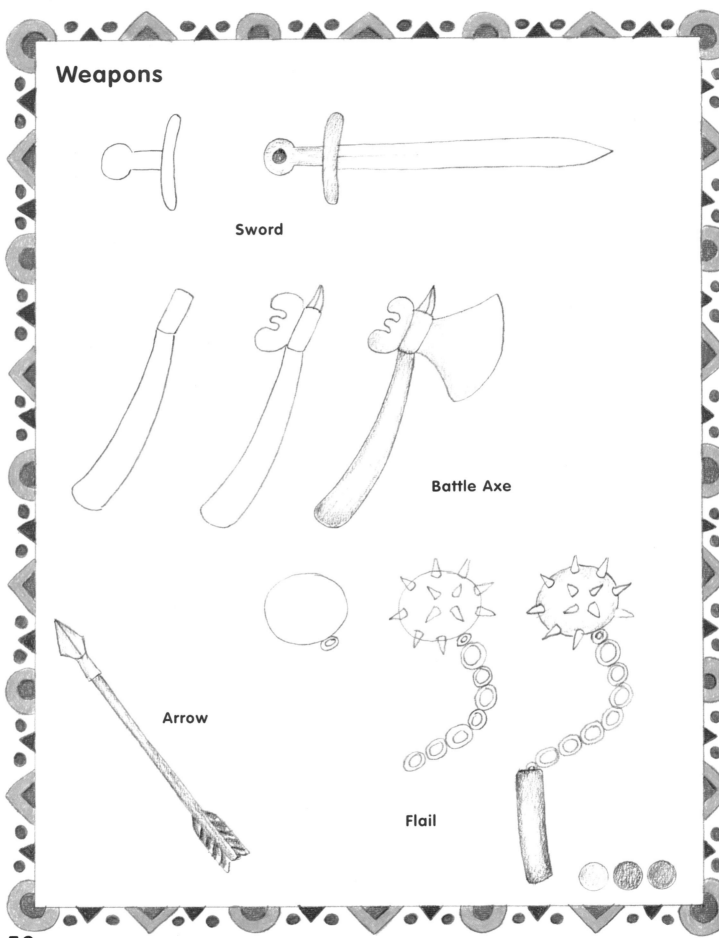

Sword

Battle Axe

Arrow

Flail

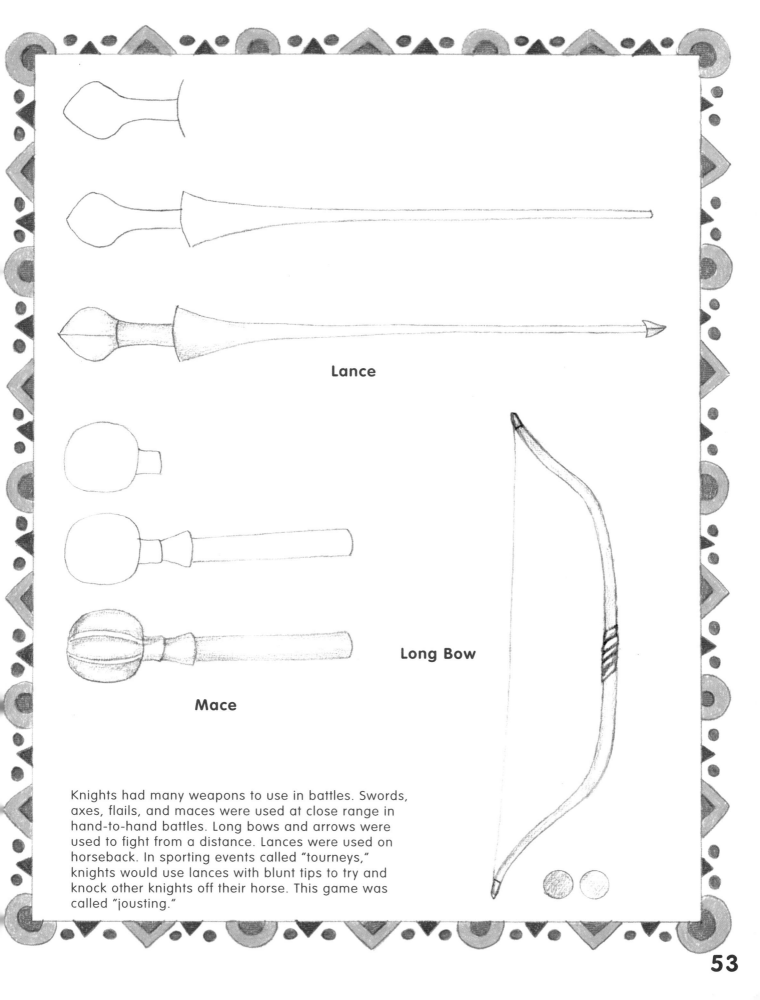

Lance

Long Bow

Mace

Knights had many weapons to use in battles. Swords, axes, flails, and maces were used at close range in hand-to-hand battles. Long bows and arrows were used to fight from a distance. Lances were used on horseback. In sporting events called "tourneys," knights would use lances with blunt tips to try and knock other knights off their horse. This game was called "jousting."

Falconry

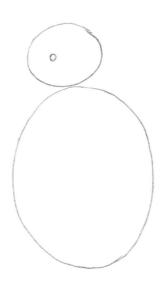

1 Sketch a **circle** and an **oval**. Add an eye.

2 Draw a beak and two folded wings.

3 Add feet and a branch.

4 LOOK at the final drawing! Draw a hood over the hawk's head. Add markings to the wings. Add claws to the feet. Erase extra lines. Shade and color.

A falconer was an expert in training birds to hunt. Falcons, hawks, and other birds of prey were specially trained. The hood on the bird's head was part of the training—it kept the bird calm. Ladies and knights would keep their favorite hawk or falcon with them and let the birds sit on the backs of their chairs during dinner.

A Page

At the age of seven, a knight's son was sent away to another castle to begin his training for knighthood. He was called a "page" and he had many duties. At mealtime, he carved meats and served the lords and ladies of the castles. He had to learn manners and how to behave respectfully. He practiced fighting skills with wooden swords. He mastered riding horses and shooting bows and arrows.

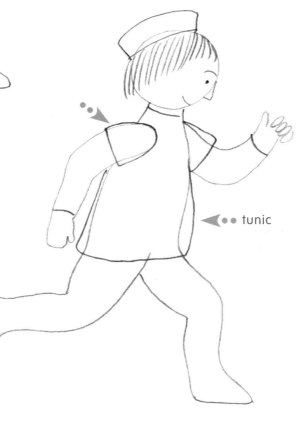

tunic

1 Start with a **basic person running** (see pages 15-16).

2 Draw a hat and hair. Add clothing lines at the neck and hands. Draw his **tunic** with short sleeves.

belt

3 Draw a **belt** on his tunic. Draw a bow and arrow in his hands. Draw lines and laces at the top of his shoes.

4 LOOK at the final drawing! Erase extra lines. Add details. Shade and color.

A Squire

When a page turned fourteen, he became a squire. He was the personal servant of a knight and traveled with him. He had many duties including cleaning and caring for the knight's armor. He had to learn to wear heavy armor and he had training in fighting skills. When he was eighteen years old, he could become a knight in a ceremony called "dubbing."

1 Start with a **basic person, front view** (see pages 5-7).

2 Draw hair lines. Add clothing lines at the neck and wrists. Draw the squire's big boots.

3 Draw his **tunic**. Add a **belt**.

tunic

4 LOOK at the final drawing. Erase extra lines. Give him a sword and shield. Add details. Don't forget his coat of arms. Shade and color.

A Minstrel

A minstrel was a traveling musician. He told stories and sang songs called ballads. Since most people in the Middle Ages could not read, this was a way they could hear stories and poems. Minstrels played many instruments including lutes, pipes, drums, and harps.

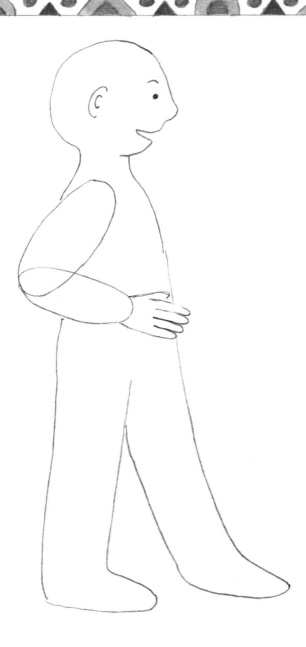

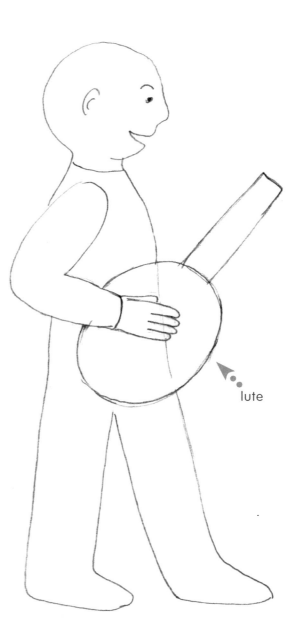

lute

1 Start with a **basic person, side view** (see pages 10-12).

2 Draw an **oval** and a **rectangle** to begin the minstrel's **lute**.

3 Draw a small **circle** inside the **oval** of the lute. Draw the tip of the neck. Add four small round pegs.

4 LOOK at the final drawing! Erase extra lines. Add details. Don't forget his hat. Shade and color.

Merry minstrel!

The Jester

The jester, or "fool," was an entertainer. He lived in the castle and was called on to amuse the lords and ladies. He juggled and told jokes and sang silly songs. Sometimes he carried a rattle with bells and sometimes a stick called a "slapstick." He wore gaudy clothes decorated with bells and colorful patches.

tunic

1   Start with your **basic person, front view** (see pages 5-7), but make the arms and legs bent at the elbows and knees.

2   Draw a jester's hat. Add bells to the points. Draw a tunic with a pointy bottom. Add clothing lines at the hands and feet.

3 Add hat lines. Draw a **rattle** in his left hand. Draw a line down the center of the tunic.

rattle

4 LOOK at the final drawing! Add the fun details. Shade and color. Don't forget the bells.

Index

Learn about other
drawing books online at
www.drawbooks.com!